*Cornerstones of Freedom*

# The Assassination of Robert F. Kennedy

Andrew Santella

**CHILDREN'S PRESS®**
A Division of Grolier Publishing
New York • London • Hong Kong • Sydney
Danbury, Connecticut

Library of Congress Cataloging-in-Publication Data

Santella, Andrew.
　The assassination of Robert F. Kennedy / by Andrew Santella.
　　p.　cm.— (Cornerstones of freedom)
　Includes index.
　Summary: Chronicles the political career of Robert F. Kennedy,
the turbulence of the United States in the 1960s, and the events that
led to Kennedy's assassination in June 1968.
　ISBN: 0-516-20790-3
　1. Kennedy, Robert F., 1925–1968—Assassination—Juvenile
literature. [1. Kennedy, Robert F., 1925–1968—Assassination.
2. United States—History—1961–1969.] I. Title. II. Series.
E840.8.K4S26　1998
364.15'24'092—dc21

　　　　　　　　　　　　　[B]　97-11342
　　　　　　　　　　　　　　　CIP
　　　　　　　　　　　　　　　AC

On June 5, 1968, Robert F. Kennedy won California's Democratic presidential primary election. A primary election is an election in which voters from each party nominate candidates for office. In the United States, there are two main political parties—the Democratic Party and the Republican Party.

It was the fourth primary election Robert Kennedy had won since he began his whirlwind race for the nomination two months earlier. It was also his most important victory yet. With his win in California, Robert F. Kennedy moved another step closer to the office that his brother John F. Kennedy had held until his tragic assassination five years earlier.

*A Kennedy campaign button*

The night after the California primary, Kennedy went to Los Angeles's Ambassador Hotel to thank his supporters and to deliver a victory speech. The crowd there was elated. The young volunteers who had worked for the

*On most of Robert F. Kennedy's campaign stops in California, he was greeted by cheering crowds.*

Kennedy campaign in California believed that their candidate was on his way to the presidency. Kennedy's speech was full of enthusiasm and hope for the future. He concluded by exclaiming, "On to Chicago," the site of the 1968 Democratic National Convention. The audience cheered wildly.

But Kennedy never made it to Chicago. And he never had the chance to put his plans for the future of the United States into practice. He was shot that night at the hotel and died a day later. The hopes of many of his supporters died with him.

*On the night Kennedy won the California Democratic primary, he delivered his victory speech at the Ambassador Hotel in Los Angeles.*

Robert F. Kennedy was born in Brookline, Massachusetts, on November 20, 1925. He grew up in a large and close-knit family. His father, Joseph P. Kennedy, was one of the richest men in the United States and held several important positions in the U.S. government. Robert, his three brothers, and his five sisters competed hard in everything from touch football games to sailboat races. They were taught to play to win. The competition wasn't limited just to games. The Kennedy children were encouraged to keep up with current events and to discuss national issues at the dinner table. The discussions sometimes became arguments.

Robert F. Kennedy's political career began in 1951 when he managed his brother John's successful campaign for the United States Senate. Robert began to earn national attention of his own in 1953 when he served as assistant counsel to the U.S. Senate subcommittee headed by Senator Joseph McCarthy. A subcommittee is a group of people who are elected or appointed to investigate certain cases. Kennedy was disturbed by McCarthy's attacks on public figures who were suspected of being Communists. After six months, Kennedy resigned. The following year (1954), he wrote a lengthy report which condemned McCarthy's actions for the committee.

*Senator Joseph McCarthy*

*Robert Kennedy (right) listens to Senator Joseph McCarthy (left) during a subcommittee hearing about suspected Communists in the United States.*

In 1957, Kennedy went to work for another Senate subcommittee that was investigating corruption (dishonesty) in labor unions such as the Teamsters. Labor unions are organizations of workers who seek to protect or improve their salaries, benefits, or working conditions. The Teamsters Union is an organization of truck drivers and other workers. Kennedy's work against corruption earned him a reputation as a determined prosecuting lawyer. But his work also made enemies of powerful men like Jimmy Hoffa, the head of the Teamsters Union.

Kennedy resigned from that committee staff in 1960 to lead his brother John's run for the presidency. Their campaign was successful. In

*John F. Kennedy's presidential inauguration was held on January 20, 1961.*

1961, John F. Kennedy was inaugurated as the country's thirty-fifth president. One of the first things John Kennedy did as president was to appoint Robert attorney general of the United States. For nearly three years, Robert F. Kennedy worked for John F. Kennedy as the nation's top law enforcement official.

Robert's appointment as attorney general was criticized by many people who believed that his only qualification for the job was being brother of the president. But Kennedy proved to be a strong attorney general. He led a tough campaign against organized crime. He gathered evidence that resulted in the conviction of Jimmy Hoffa. It was one of his proudest achievements.

*As U.S. attorney general, Robert (center) often visited the White House to discuss policies with his brother John (right) and Vice President Lyndon Johnson (left).*

*During the upheaval of the 1960s, anti-Vietnam War protests took place throughout the country.*

Kennedy also worked to see that the laws of the nation helped to improve the lives of ordinary people. The 1960s were a time of tremendous upheaval in the United States. The nation was divided over its involvement in the war in Vietnam. Racial unrest led to rioting in cities such as Washington, D.C., Detroit, and Los Angeles. As African-Americans increasingly demanded their civil rights, Kennedy used the power of the United States government to protect them from often unsympathetic local authorities. He intervened to protect black students who were attending the universities

of Alabama and Mississippi. He sent four hundred federal marshals to guard Martin Luther King Jr. and his supporters from an angry mob in Mobile, Alabama. And he proposed the Civil Rights Act of 1964, which banned discrimination in voting, jobs, and public accommodations (hotels, restrooms, or waiting rooms).

*Top: Attorney General Robert Kennedy worked with African-Americans to settle the racial problems that were occurring in cities throughout the country.*

*Left: When Alabama governor George Wallace (third from right) refused to admit two African-American students to the University of Alabama in Tuscaloosa, Robert Kennedy sent federal marshals there to settle the tense situation.*

Unfortunately, the Civil Rights Act was passed into law only after President John Kennedy's assassination on November 22, 1963. Working together, the Kennedy brothers had achieved a great deal. But that was small consolation to Robert in the sad days after the president was killed.

Robert Kennedy was devasted by John's death. He spent long periods simply staring out windows or walking in the woods. When he finally was able to resume his career, he did so with such energy and compassion that many people considered him to be a hero.

*President John F. Kennedy's burial in Arlington National Cemetery took place on November 25, 1963.*

Robert Kennedy served as attorney general in the cabinet of President Lyndon Johnson, who succeeded John Kennedy in 1963. From the beginning, Robert Kennedy's relationship with Johnson was strained. After a few months, Kennedy resigned. He received high praise for the work he did as the country's attorney general. In an editorial, the *New York Times,* which had criticized his appointment three years earlier, said Kennedy "put new vigor into protecting civil rights through administrative action [and] played a pivotal role in shaping the most comprehensive civil rights law in this country."

*Lyndon Johnson was sworn in as president of the United States just hours after John Kennedy died. Next to Johnson is Jaqueline Kennedy, widow of John Kennedy.*

*Robert Kennedy addressed a crowd of well-wishers following the announcement of his resignation from the office of attorney general.*

Even though he resigned from his post as attorney general, Kennedy did not retire from politics. He campaigned for the U.S. Senate seat from New York and was elected easily in 1964. As a senator, he remained a champion of social reform. He supported President Johnson's efforts to eliminate poverty and to guarantee the civil rights of minorities. But he also criticized the president's policies on the war in Vietnam.

For years, the United States had been sending more and more soldiers to help the South Vietnamese government to fight Communist North Vietnam. Yet many Americans believed that victory was impossible. Even though John Kennedy had increased U.S. involvement in

*As a senator, Robert worked to improve the lives of poor people. Here, he donates twenty-nine pairs of shoes that he collected from his own nine children to a children's charity.*

Vietnam while he was president, Robert Kennedy believed that the U.S. military should withdraw. As he continued to challenge President Johnson on this issue, Kennedy's supporters began to urge him to run for president in 1968.

On March 16 of that year, Robert F. Kennedy announced that he would run for the presidency. He said that he was running "to seek new policies, policies to end the bloodshed in Vietnam and in our cities, policies to close the gap that now exists between black and white." For the rest of his campaign, Kennedy often returned to these themes of racial justice and an end to the war in Vietnam.

On March 18, he delivered a major speech about Vietnam. He criticized President Johnson's handling of the war. At the same time, he accepted his share of the blame for mistakes the Kennedy administration had made. But, he said, the time had come to learn from those mistakes. He called the war a "bottomless pit" that was destroying "the spirit of our country." "This is a year of choice," he said. "A year when we choose not simply who will lead us, but where we wish to be led. . . . I am concerned that our present course will not bring victory, will not bring peace. . . . I am concerned that at the end of it all, there will only be more Americans killed."

*On the presidential campaign trail, Robert enjoyed greeting the crowds of supporters who came to hear him speak.*

Two weeks after Kennedy's speech, President Johnson announced that he would not seek reelection. The path seemed to be clear for Robert F. Kennedy to make his run for the White House.

*Martin Luther King Jr. was a leading voice for racial equality in this country. His "I Have a Dream" speech is considered one of the most famous speeches in United States history.*

Then, as it did so often in the 1960s, tragedy struck. On April 4, 1968, Martin Luther King Jr. was assassinated in Memphis, Tennessee. Kennedy was scheduled to speak that night in a poor, black neighborhood of Indianapolis, Indiana. King's murder was a crushing blow to African-Americans who had counted on King to lead them in their struggle for civil rights. Police officials expected that grief and anger over the killing would result in rioting in some cities. They warned Kennedy that it might not be safe for him to visit the Indianapolis neighborhood. But Kennedy wouldn't be talked out of it.

*As Kennedy got off a plane in Indianapolis, Indiana, his expression reflected the sadness he felt upon hearing the news of Martin Luther King Jr.'s murder.*

When Kennedy arrived, he realized that his audience had not yet learned of King's assassination. He broke the news to them. Then, as he had in his speech on Vietnam, he offered them a choice. "You can be filled with bitterness, with hatred, and a desire for revenge. . . . Or we can make an effort, as Martin Luther King did . . . to replace that violence, that stain of bloodshed that has spread across the land, with an effort to understand with compassion and love."

He ended his speech by reminding the audience that he, too, had experienced loss when his brother was killed. He told them that he understood the feeling of bitterness. But he urged them to join him and "go beyond these rather difficult times." It was a remarkable speech for a politician. It wasn't about policies, or laws, or campaigns. It was an appeal to the goodness of the American people during a crisis. Kennedy's speeches about Vietnam and Martin Luther King

Jr. showed his leadership and compassion. As the presidential campaign went on, many voters turned to Kennedy for those very qualities.

Still, the nation's worst fears came true in the days following King's assassination. African-American rioters and looters took to the streets in cities all over the United States. In Washington, D.C., a thick curtain of smoke from arson fires hung over the White House and the Capitol. By the end of the week that King died, the riots had taken thirty-seven lives and destroyed millions of dollars of property.

*These buildings in Washington, D.C., were destroyed by fires set by angry African-Americans who rioted for days following King's death.*

In the weeks that followed, Kennedy spoke throughout the country. Large, enthusiastic crowds greeted him on college campuses and in big cities. They also came out to vote for him, helping him win primary elections that spring in Nebraska, Indiana, the District of Columbia, and South Dakota.

By June, the stage was set for the crucial primary election in California. If Kennedy could win there, he would become the clear front-runner for the Democratic nomination. Kennedy was hugely popular with African-American and Mexican-American voters in California. Many of them believed that Kennedy understood their concerns better than any other candidate from either party.

Kennedy had always been an intense campaigner. He approached his political life the same way he had been taught as a boy to approach any competition—with a determination to win. Kennedy campaigned tirelessly, traveling up and down the state. Although he was mobbed by admirers in some places, he was jeered in other places. But Kennedy kept on campaigning. Soon, though, the hard work began to take its toll on him. During a speech in San Diego, Kennedy became so ill that he had to stop speaking. But soon, the reporters who followed his campaign began to notice a change in Kennedy. He was loosening up, cracking jokes, and having more fun.

*Kennedy takes time out to relax with one of his children and the family dog, Freckles.*

On June 4, two months after the tragedy of the King assassination, the voters helped to carry Kennedy to a convincing victory in the California Democratic primary. He won forty-six percent of the vote.

Kennedy spent the day of the primary resting. He went to the Malibu, California, home of movie director John Frankenheimer, a Kennedy supporter, to swim and lounge by the ocean.

While Kennedy was relaxing, Frankenheimer's twelve-year-old son David was playing in the surf. Suddenly, an enormous wave caught David and pulled him under the water's surface. Kennedy rushed into the ocean to save the boy. In the process of pulling him from the water, Kennedy cut himself over one eye.

Kennedy hoped to address the media in Malibu that night, instead of going to Los Angeles for the usual post-election press conference. His campaign staff even rented some of the electronic equipment reporters would need and brought it to Frankenheimer's house. But several television networks insisted that the press conference take place in Los Angeles. So Kennedy and his aides rushed to get ready for the appearance. Frankenheimer used a little of his wife's makeup in an attempt to disguise the cut over Kennedy's eye. Then the candidate and his friends jumped into a car and sped into the city.

A large, enthusiastic crowd waited for Kennedy in the ballroom of the Ambassador Hotel. Early election returns suggested a victory for Kennedy. The volunteers who had worked so hard for that result were ready to celebrate. Once Kennedy declared the victory, they were even more ecstatic.

Kennedy loved crowds like the one at the Ambassador Hotel. He liked to walk into the mass of people, shaking hands, and thanking the people who had turned out to support him. But the ballroom was simply too packed with people. There seemed to be no way to wade through the crush of well-wishers. So his aides led Kennedy out of the ballroom by an alternate route. It was a fatal decision.

*On the night he won the California Democratic primary, Robert and his wife Ethel greeted hundreds of supporters at the Ambassador Hotel in Los Angeles, California.*

Kennedy, in the middle of a group of friends, reporters, and campaign staff exited into a narrow hallway and through a set of swinging doors. These doors led into the pantry of the hotel's kitchen. There, Kennedy stopped to shake hands with two hotel workers, Jesus Perez and Juan Romero. As he shook hands with Romero, shots rang out. Kennedy's hand went limp. Romero felt warm blood when he reached for the candidate's arm.

Sirhan Bishara Sirhan, a twenty-four-year-old Arab immigrant from Jordan, had been standing against one wall of the kitchen. As Kennedy made his way through, Sirhan approached him, pulled out a .22 caliber pistol, and shot him three times from point blank range. Then he sprayed the room with more gunfire, wounding five other people.

*After Kennedy's speech, he was led through the door at the rear into the hotel kitchen's pantry. The "X" in the foreground is the spot where Kennedy fell after he was shot.*

Finally, Kennedy supporters grabbed Sirhan and overpowered him. One wrenched the weapon from his hand. Some of the people tried to attack Sirhan, while others rushed to Kennedy's side. But the damage was already done. Kennedy lay on the floor of the kitchen in a pool of blood. Someone loosened his shirt. Romero tried to give his rosary to Kennedy, but by then Kennedy was too weak to hold it. A friend of the Kennedy family took off his coat and placed it under Kennedy's head. A reporter cleared a path for Ethel Kennedy to get to her wounded husband. Shaking, she crouched down to him, whispered a few words, then stood and asked the crowd to step back. An ambulance arrived to rush the senator to The Hospital of the Good Samaritan.

*Sirhan Sirhan (center) is led away by police following the shooting.*

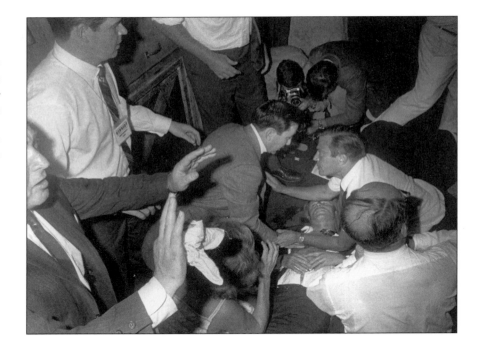

*In the chaos that followed the shooting, Senator Kennedy lies on the floor of the pantry, as Ethel (at bottom) kneels beside him.*

*Reporters read the morning newspaper as they wait outside The Hospital of the Good Samaritan for word on Kennedy's condition.*

At the hospital, a priest administered Last Rites, a sacrament in the Roman Catholic Church in which a dying person is blessed. Kennedy's wife sat by his side, holding his hand. He underwent emergency surgery for the most serious of his wounds—a bullet that had lodged in the middle of his brain. For a time, doctors held out hope that Kennedy could be saved. But in the early morning hours of June 6, he died.

On June 8, President Johnson and Vice President Hubert Humphrey, along with the other

26

presidential candidates, joined the Kennedy family at St. Patrick's Cathedral in New York City for the funeral service. From there, the casket carrying Kennedy's body traveled by funeral train to Washington, D.C. Mourners lined the tracks. People held up signs that read, "We love you, Bobby" and "We'll miss you." Ordinary people filled every train station along the way.

Once in the nation's capital, Kennedy's body was taken by motorcade to Arlington National Cemetery. He was buried at night just down a hillside from his brother John. Thousands of candles lit the scene. Some mourners felt that the candles were bringing light to the darkness, just as Robert Kennedy had brought light to the United States in some of its darkest hours.

*Kennedy's flag-draped casket, surrounded by candles, during his funeral service at St. Patrick's Cathedral in New York City*

*Sirhan Sirhan continues to serve his life sentence for the murder of Robert Kennedy.*

On the night of the assassination, Sirhan Sirhan had been captured in the kitchen of the Ambassador Hotel. He confessed to killing Robert Kennedy. He said that he was bitter because of Kennedy's support for Israel, the nation Sirhan regarded as the enemy of all Arab people. In 1969, he was brought to trial and convicted of murder.

In the years since Kennedy's assassination, several investigators have questioned whether Sirhan was the real killer. They believe that he was brainwashed and set up to take the blame for the killing while the true murderers walked free. Even some police and FBI agents have challenged the official version of events. They believe that the Los Angeles police made too many mistakes in their original investigation. They point to differing versions of eyewitness testimony about how many shots were fired and from what location in the hotel pantry.

None of these issues was raised at Sirhan's trial. The jury convicted him of murder and he was sentenced to death. Later, that sentence was reduced to life imprisonment. Sirhan is still serving his sentence in a California prison. Whatever the facts about Sirhan, one truth remains unchanged: Robert Kennedy never got the chance to offer his hopeful vision of the future as the president of the United States.

Still, Kennedy's high standards are kept alive in his honor. He believed that anyone who "stands up for an ideal, or acts to improve the lot of others, or strikes out against injustice" could help to change the world. Those who share his belief continue his work.

*Today, a simple white cross marks the gravesite of Robert F. Kennedy. Each year, thousands of people visit Kennedy's grave to honor him and the ideals he stood for.*

# GLOSSARY

**brainwash** – to change someone's beliefs or actions against their will

**civil rights** – rights to personal freedom that were established by the U.S. Constitution and by acts of Congress

**Communist** – person who belongs to the Communist Party or believes in a system of government based on sharing property in common

**counsel** – adviser in legal matters

**intervene** – to come between two sides who disagree to help solve a problem

**marshal** – law officer who performs duties similar to those of a sheriff

**motorcade** – procession or parade of cars

**national convention** – meeting of the national political parties held just before presidential elections, to determine and announce candidates and policies

**protest** – demonstration or statement against something

**rosary** – string of beads used in the Roman Catholic Church for counting prayers

**sentence** – punishment to be inflicted upon a convicted criminal

**whirlwind** – very quick and sudden

*marshal*

*protest*

# TIMELINE

**1925** *November 20:* Robert F. Kennedy born

**1951** Manages successful U.S. Senate campaign
for John F. Kennedy

**1953**

Assistant counsel to
McCarthy's subcommittee

**1957** Chief counsel to committee
investigating labor unions

Manages John F. Kennedy's
presidential campaign

**1960**

**1961** Named U.S. attorney general

*November 22:* John F. Kennedy assassinated **1963**

Wins U.S. Senate seat **1964**

**1968**

*March 16:*
Announces
campaign for
presidency

Sirhan sentenced to life imprisonment **1969**

*April 4:* King assassinated

*June 5:* Wins California Democratic
primary; shot at Ambassador Hotel

*June 6:* Dies at Good
Samaritan Hospital

## INDEX *(Boldface page numbers indicate illustrations.)*

## PHOTO CREDITS

©: AP/Wide World Photos: 1, 9, 18, 19, 20, 26, 28, 29, 31 bottom left; Archive Photos: cover, 4, 7 top, 10, 12, 15, 16, 21, 27, 30 bottom, 31 top right; Archive Photos/American Stock: 17; Archive Photos/Blank Archives: 3, 31 bottom right; Archive Photos/Consolidated News: 8, 13; UPI/Corbis-Bettmann: 2, 5, 6, 7 bottom, 11, 14, 23, 24, 25, 26 top, 30 top, 31 top left.

## ABOUT THE AUTHOR

Andrew Santella is a lifelong resident of Chicago. He is a graduate of Chicago's Loyola University, where he studied American literature. He writes about history, sports, and popular culture for several magazines for young people. He is the author of these other Children's Press titles: *The Battle of the Alamo, The Capitol,* and *Jackie Robinson Breaks the Color Line* (Cornerstones of Freedom) and *Mo Vaughn* (Sports Stars).